Mackinac Island

*M*ackinac Island represents an era past where no automobiles are allowed and horse-drawn carriages and bicycles are the mode of transportation.

The Grand Hotel has stood overlooking the Straits of Mackinac for over a century, and a visit to the hotel is an unforgettable experience.

The Round Island Lighthouse is a well recognized landmark by those traveling to Mackinac Island by ferry.

▲ Cedarville

▲ De Tour Village

*H*ighway M-134 passes along the exquisite shoreline to Cedarville and on to De Tour Village.
Les Cheneaux Islands, a French term meaning "The Channels," is descriptive of the waterways separating a group of 36 islands east of the Straits of Mackinac. The Les Cheneaux Islands Antique Wooden Boat Show, held each year in Hessel, has been a center of attraction since it began in 1976.
Looking toward Drummond Island, a Great Lakes ore carrier can be seen silently passing behind the two red and white fishing boats in the foreground.

Point Iroquois Light Station is located five miles west of Brimley.

*T*he locks at Sault Ste. Marie allow ships sailing between Lake Superior and Lake Huron to by-pass the rapids on the St. Mary's River. It takes only a few minutes to raise or lower huge ships the 21 foot difference between the lake levels.

Soo Locks

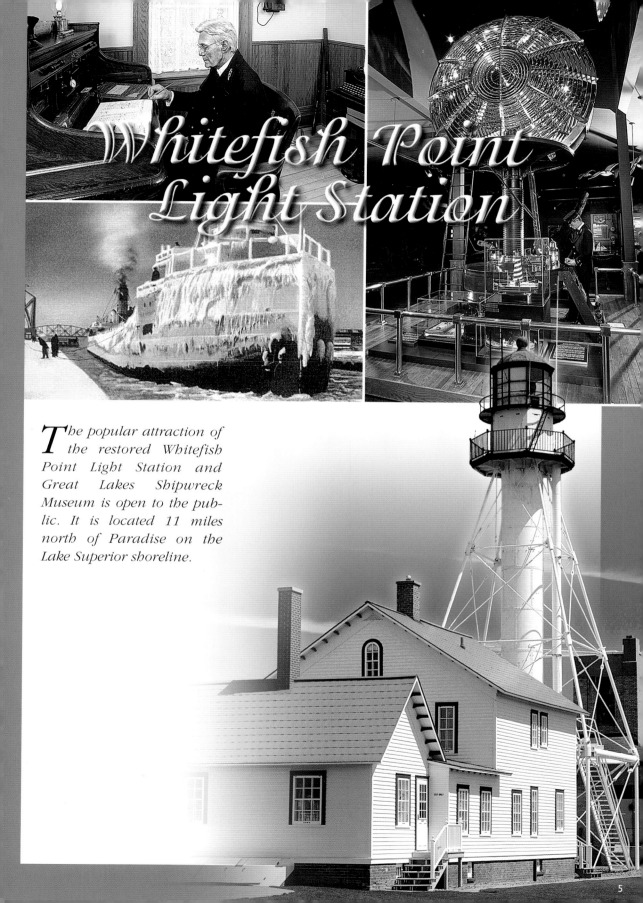

Whitefish Point Light Station

*T*he popular attraction of the restored Whitefish Point Light Station and Great Lakes Shipwreck Museum is open to the public. It is located 11 miles north of Paradise on the Lake Superior shoreline.

The Tahquamenon Falls, located between Paradise and Newberry in the Tahquamenon Falls State Park, is divided into the Upper and Lower Falls. Water drained from the swampland acquires tannic acid giving it an amber color during the rainy seasons, while in the dry seasons it is white.

The Upper Falls is the largest falls east of the Mississippi and plunges 48 feet in one huge wall of thundering splendor over a curving rock ledge. Several overlooks, with outstanding pictorial vantage points along the path, lead to the brink.

At the Lower Falls, four miles down stream, the river separates forming an island with cascading waterfalls on either side. The scenic island can easily be reached by a short rowboat trip.

Photo: Henri Spiris

Tahquamenon Falls

*A*long the region between Grand Marais and Munising there are many areas of outstanding beauty and interest.

The Au Sable Point Lighthouse, with associated keeper's quarters, is located along Lake Superior's rugged shoreline in the Pictured Rocks National Lakeshore. The remains of an ancient shipwreck can still be seen on the shoreline testifying to the dangers of stormy waters.

Grand Sable Dunes and Grand Sable Falls are two of the many scenic spots visitors enjoy in this area.

Pictured Rocks

*T*he abandoned Grand Island Lighthouse and many spectacular rock formations, some rising from the water to a height of 200 feet, can be viewed by visitors on the Pictured Rocks Cruise Boats operating from Munising.

Wagner Falls is a short walk along a delightful path in the Munising area.

The Munising Falls flows over the rim of a huge stone cavern to a drop of about 72 feet.

*L*ocated at the village of Christmas, the historic Bay Furnace was in service smelting ore from 1870 to 1877.

Munising Falls

Wagner Falls

*M*arquette, the principal city of the Upper Peninsula, is a center for travel, education and commerce. Founded along the rocky shore of Lake Superior, it is named in honor of Father Jacques Marquette, the famous canoe voyager and missionary who was a prominent figure in Northern Michigan history.

The discovery of rich iron ore deposits, just west of Marquette, in the mid 1800's played an important role in the development of this community.

Iron mining is still one of the important industries in the Upper Peninsula. Ore is transported from the iron range, by rail, to loading docks where Great Lakes freighters then deliver it to ports in several states.

The first Marquette Harbor Lighthouse was established in 1853. In 1866 a square forty foot masonry tower replaced it and still serves to this day.

Houghton-Hancock

*B*ishop Baraga Shrine overlooks the Keweenaw Bay between L'Anse and Baraga. Over 100 years ago Bishop Baraga, often called the "Snowshoe Priest," was famous for missionary work among the Indians.

*T*he Quincy Lookout on U.S. 41 at Hancock provides this spectacular overlook. Winter activities here are very popular and this dog team is ready for action.

*C*anyon Falls is located on the Sturgeon River south of L'Anse.

Passenger service is provided between Isle Royale National Park and Houghton-Hancock. These sister cities stand facing each other on steep hillsides overlooking Portage Lake, and are connected by the Vertical Lift Bridge.

Copper mines were scattered throughout the region as this early photo of copper miners loading ore depicts.

*T*he Delaware Mine was active from 1847 to 1887. This educational and interesting attraction is on U.S. 41, between Calumet and Copper Harbor, in Michigan's Copper Country.

Lake Superior

*L*ake Superior presents an ever-changing panorama of beauty. Sometimes it is rugged and rocky, sometimes peaceful and tranquil, but always interesting and exciting.

*J*ust north of Houghton-Hancock, Quincy Mine and Steam Hoist has long been a landmark. Now part of the Keweenaw National Historical Park, it is open to the public for tours. Built in 1920 and operating until 1931, the steam hoist was the largest steam-powered mine hoist ever built, bringing copper ore from 9,260 feet on the incline and 5,640 feet vertically.

Copper Country

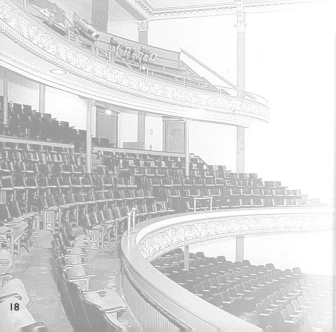

*T*he Calumet Theatre, an addition to the town hall, opened in 1900 and became one of the finest municipal theaters in America. It has been designated as a National Historic Landmark and is one of the Upper Peninsula's unique attractions. Seating 700, it is still in use with regularly scheduled productions as well as tours.

*T*he Copper Harbor Lighthouse is located at the tip of the Keweenaw Peninsula along the rugged Lake Superior shoreline. Manitou Island Lighthouse stands just off the tip of the Keweenaw Peninsula. Isle Royale National Park, America's only island park, is located on Lake Superior, 48 miles north of Copper Harbor.

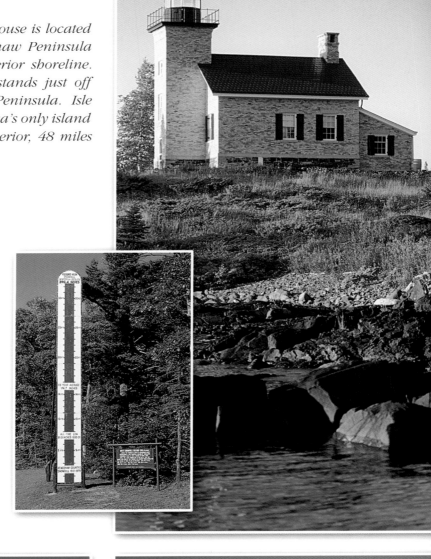

The marker on Highway 41 between Houghton-Hancock and Copper Harbor graphically depicts the record snowfall of 1978-79 which was 390.4 inches!

Brightly colored lichen covers the rocks in both the Manitou Island Lighthouse and Isle Royale photos.

*F*rom Brockway Mountain Drive gorgeous views overlooking Lake Superior, Copper Harbor and Lake Fanny Hooe can be seen.

Fort Wilkins was constructed in 1844 to maintain peace during the period of Michigan's copper boom. The historic fort is in Fort Wilkins State Park, at Copper Harbor on the shores of Lake Fanny Hooe.

Eagle Harbor Lighthouse stands on a rocky point at the harbor entrance on Lake Superior. The first lighthouse was built here in 1851, but was replaced in 1871 by this structure.

*S*and Hills Lighthouse, built in 1917 located at "Five Mile Point" on Lake Superior, warns vessels away from Sawtooth Reef. It is now open year 'round as a Bed & Breakfast Inn.

*B*ears are quite common in Michigan and while by nature are shy, visitors should be cautious. When a cub is seen, one can be sure mother bear is close by and she is extremely protective.

*O*ntonagon Lighthouse, built in 1866-67, is a yellow brick tower with attached keeper's quarters. It stands along the Ontonagon River at Ontonagon.

This view (top photo) was taken at the western most point of Michigan. Here, the Montreal River divides Michigan and Wisconsin at Lake Superior not far from Little Girl's Point.

Copper Peak, the only ski flying hill in the Western Hemisphere, is just north of Bessemer. Ski flyers from throughout the world compete at this site.

Ironwood 1886

"Ironwood"

*L*ocated at the westernmost end of the Upper Peninsula, Ironwood greets visitors entering Michigan from the west. The town's growth is depicted by the difference in the photos from 1886 to the present.

Wakefield, located along the shores of beautiful Sunday Lake, was an important iron mining center. It is a picturesque village in this western Upper Peninsula recreational area.

Nee-Gaw-Nee-Gaw-Bow (Leading Man,) a huge wooden sculpture overlooking Sunday Lake at U.S. 2 and M-28 in Wakefield, is the 60th statue of Peter Wolf Toth's "Trail of the Whispering Giants" honoring Native Americans.

Wakefield

*T*he Cornish Pump
Museum and Fumee
Creek Waterfall are two of
Iron Mountain's landmarks
pictured here. The pump,
built in 1890, stands 54
feet high, weighs 160 tons,
and could pump water at a
rate of 3,000 gallons per
minute from iron mines
1500 feet deep.

*B*ond Falls is located
near Paulding
between Bruce Crossing
and Watersmeet.

Bond Falls

Escanaba

Gladstone Harbor

E scanaba, located on Little Bay de Noc, is an important ore shipping port and vacation center. The picturesque waterfront, large yacht harbor, causeway drive to the beach and spacious park area provide inviting recreational facilities for residents and visitors.

Gladstone Harbor provides excellent marina facilities for visitors and residents as well as access to Little Bay de Noc, Green Bay, Lake Michigan and connecting waterways. Soo Line Engine 730, built in 1911, stands as a memorial to the era of steam railroading, which ended in 1956.

Menominee-
Marinette

*T*he Menominee River, separating Michigan and Wisconsin at the twin cities of Menominee-Marinette, flows past the Menominee Lighthouse and empties into Green Bay. The Tourist Welcome Center greets visitors entering Michigan from Wisconsin.

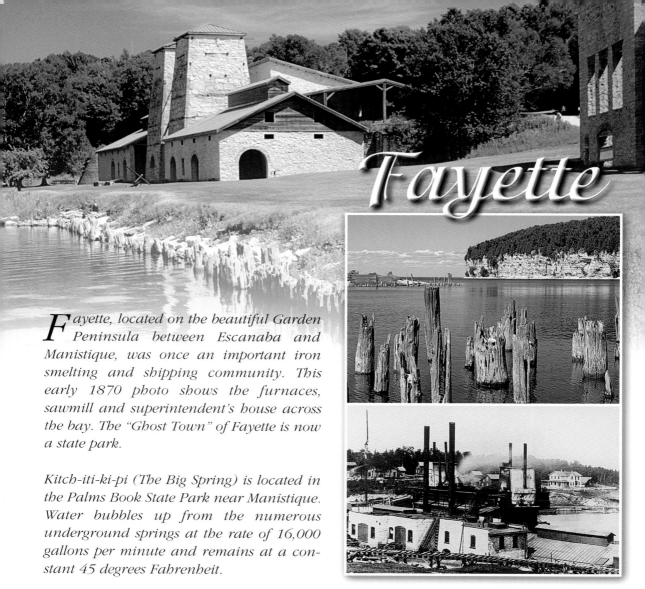

Fayette

*F*ayette, located on the beautiful Garden Peninsula between Escanaba and Manistique, was once an important iron smelting and shipping community. This early 1870 photo shows the furnaces, sawmill and superintendent's house across the bay. The "Ghost Town" of Fayette is now a state park.

Kitch-iti-ki-pi (The Big Spring) is located in the Palms Book State Park near Manistique. Water bubbles up from the numerous underground springs at the rate of 16,000 gallons per minute and remains at a constant 45 degrees Fahrenheit.

Kitch-iti-ki-pi

*H*istoric Manistique, home of the famous Paul Bunyan, is a pleasant community and port city along the Lake Michigan shoreline.

Manistique

Manistique's Water Tower, a Roman period architectural landmark built in 1922, is located in Pioneer Park along with a log cabin and home of early residents of Schoolcraft county.

*S*eney National Wildlife Refuge protects an environment that was developed to provide nesting habitat for many species of waterfowl and other wildlife. This system covers 95,455 acres with over 7,000 acres of open water in 21 major pools. A visitor and information center, miles of scenic drives and nature trails are available as well as fishing in certain selected areas.

For many miles U.S. 2, between Naubinway and St. Ignace, follows close to the waters edge offering travelers many lovely panoramic views of the northern shore of Lake Michigan. The Cut River Bridge is one of these choice locations.

The Museum of Ojibwa Culture, a national historic landmark and the grave of Father Marquette are both located in the St. Ignace area.

Naubinway, the largest commercial fishing port on the Great Lakes, is the northernmost community on the Lake Michigan shoreline.

Imp Lake